(Make this book a spec~~ial~~
to someone

Presented to

_____

By

_____

Date

_____

Occasion

_____

THE LESSONS OF CHELBY

THE LESSONS OF CHELBY

A Real Life Story

Whether you are on a 'living life to its fullest' high
or are going through the challenge of your life, stay
tuned and GET READY!

BRENDA ANDERSON PARKER

authorHOUSE®

AuthorHouse™
1663 Liberty Drive
Bloomington, IN 47403
www.authorhouse.com
Phone: 1-800-839-8640

First published by AuthorHouse   10/25/2011

ISBN: 978-1-4634-3093-1 (sc)
ISBN: 978-1-4634-3092-4 (ebk)

Library of Congress Control Number: 2011911962

Printed in the United States of America

Any people depicted in stock imagery provided by Thinkstock are models, and such images are being used for illustrative purposes only.
Certain stock imagery © Thinkstock.

This book is printed on acid-free paper.

CONTENTS

ACKNOWLEDGEMENTS.. ix

SPECIAL ACKNOWLEDGEMENT xi

    Dr. Dale Swift Pediatric Neurosurgeon xi

Chapter 1   Living Life to the Fullest 1

Chapter 2   A Cold Morning in January.............................. 4

Chapter 3   How Quickly Things Can Change!....................... 7

Chapter 4   My Talk with God... 12

Chapter 5   We Don't Need Sympathy 16

Chapter 6   Challenge, After Challenge, After Challenge! 20

Chapter 7   The Warrior in Chelby..................................... 25

Chapter 8   Confident, Even When Trouble is Near 28

Chapter 9   The Decision 32

Chapter 10   A New Beginning 35

Chapter 11   My AH-HA Moment 38

Chapter 12   She Shall Live and Not Die............................. 42

Chapter 13   Our "Warrior Princess"(From The Parent's Perspective)............. 46

Chapter 14   Chelby My Chelby(by Chelby's Oldest Sister Chantel).............. 54

Chapter 15   Our Father Will Be There When We Get There 59

APPENDIX 65

    Chelby's Medical History 67

    DAILY AFFIRMATIONS... 69

    ALWAYS REMEMBER... 71

AUTHOR'S BIOGRAPHY 73

ACKNOWLEDGEMENTS

First I want to thank the Lord God Almighty for my assignment to bring this story to the world. The spirit of the Lord said that millions will be blessed by Chelby's story.

Next, I want to thank Chelby's immediate family, Roy, Chijuana, Chantel, and Chayse for their support and allowing me to use their lives to encourage others. Sometimes God gives us an assignment which may at times be very challenging, but He sends us just what we need. Thanks to James and Lucille Anderson, James, Jr. and Lynn Anderson, Merco Parker, Shirley Singleton and Verla Emery for their grand support.

A special thanks to Johnnie Sanders, a very phenomenal friend and advisor who was instructed by the spirit to coach me through to completion of this book. I will always remember how you continued to be the encourager that you have always been. Thank you, Johnnie.

Finally, a very big thank you to my sisters and brothers in Christ, many friends, co-workers and associates from the east to the west coasts who prayed; never giving up on what God has for our baby girl and "The Lessons of Chelby". THANK YOU LORD!

SPECIAL ACKNOWLEDGEMENT

Dr. Dale Swift
Pediatric Neurosurgeon

There are no words on earth that could express our gratitude for what God does through Dr. Swift for Chelby and others. I remember her first stroke. Our family was extremely concerned. Not knowing which way to turn or what to do, I called Dr. Ben Carson's office at John Hopkins University Hospital seeking help. I was told that he was not handling pediatric AVMs. A colleague of Dr. Carson asked me the name of the surgeon working with the baby. I told him Dr. Swift. He stated that Dr. Swift is the best in the NATION. Praise God, He had already given us the BEST. Thank you, Lord and thank you, Dr. Swift.

Chapter 1

Living Life to the Fullest

Most of us have to deal with a lot these days. With the loss of jobs, loved ones, homes, and troubling happenings around the world, the **POWER** to **PUSH** through to success is absolutely necessary. This begs the question, "How do we *P ray U ntil S omething H appens?*"

How do we push through so many difficulties and troubles? How do we hold on to an attitude of "*I can do all things through Christ who strengthens me?*" We know studies have shown that medical illnesses are derived from stress associated with negative thinking and low self-esteem issues. How do we keep a positive mental outlook, so that circumstances won't drive us to losing our cool? How do we keep it all together and move forward?

This book was created especially for **YOU and ME!** My hope is that it will provide inspirational thoughts for every challenging situation, and every experience that may occur in LIFE. I pray this book will help inspire and motivate us to live life to its fullest.

Hopefully, the nuggets of gold in **The Lessons of Chelby** will serve to help us stay focused on what's most important in life—being in the **PRESENCE** of all there is—God's LOVE! Use my inspired nuggets of gold every time you have a challenge, or just when you're on top of the world and want to remain there.

Sure, there will be demanding days from time to time. I hope you will remember to pick up **The Lessons of Chelby** *(in audio or the book form)* and move inward to the center of your being. This is where you can have a simple encounter with spiritual metamorphosis that will propel you to **PUSH.** This happens to Chelby every morning when she wakes up and shouts with a sense of entitlement *"IS IT WAKE UP TIME!"*

Inspirational Nugget Of Gold—Lesson #1
Created by the guidance of the Holy Spirit!

My child, yes it is time to get up! Today remember: *"When you want what you've never had before, you will be required to do what you've never done before."* This thought will give you the attitude necessary to win in any situation and any circumstance.

Create something new and different.

P.S. In the space below, create your own nugget(s) of gold to inspire you to stay centered in the spirit of . . . *YES! IT IS TIME TO WAKE UP, TO GET UP AND TO MOVE UP.*

Create your own nugget(s) of gold

_____
_____
_____
_____
_____
_____
_____
_____
_____

Chapter 2

A Cold Morning in January

It was Thursday, the 23rd of January in 2003 and it was a ve—ry cold morning in Dallas, Texas. Even though my daughter Chijuana had been hospitalized and restricted to bed rest for three months, our family felt life was absolutely wonderful! Chijuana was eight months pregnant with her third child. She was already the mother of two beautiful girls: Chantel and Chelby.

My mother was visiting from Louisiana; she and I were watching Chelby, our 19-month old baby girl; model her new fleece leopard jacket. Chelby was so excited about her new outfit; she was twirling around like a princess. Shortly after our impromptu fashion show, Chijuana's husband, Roy, took Chelby to the babysitter. It was a typical week day morning—so we thought.

About noon, Chijuana received a call from the babysitter telling her that Chelby had fallen and may need to see a doctor. Since Chijuana was on bed rest, she called me at work and asked me if I could pick Chelby up from the babysitter. I said yes, however, I was not able to leave right away. An hour later I called my daughter to see how Chelby was doing; the babysitter had called and said Chelby was fine. She had eaten lunch and was taking an afternoon nap.

Approximately 45 minutes later, the babysitter called my daughter again. This time her voice sounded frantic. "Chelby doesn't look like Chelby; she looks as if she's in pain and I cannot wake her up. I'm taking her to Baylor Hospital's emergency room down the street from my house."

"Is Chelby breathing?" Chijuana asked hysterically. The babysitter dropped the telephone receiver without answering. Chijuana started screaming and crying.

Inspirational Nugget Of Gold—Lesson #2
Created by the guidance of the Holy Spirit!

There have been times in our lives that we felt/feel life was/is absolutely wonderful; life is good, we might say! Suddenly, something happens to change the very essence of our peace and joy. Just remember, ***"No weapon formed against us shall prosper." Isaiah 54:17.*** In other words, God never said problems would not come, He never said they would not show up, but He did say that they will not overtake you.

Create something new and different.

P.S. In the space below, create your own nugget(s) of gold to inspire you to stay centered in the spirit of . . .

NO CHALLENGE SHALL PREVAIL OVER ME!

_____

Create your own nugget(s) of gold

_____
_____
_____
_____
_____
_____
_____
_____
_____
_____
_____
_____
_____
_____
_____
_____
_____
_____

Chapter 3

How Quickly Things Can Change!

After many failed attempts, Chijuana was finally able to contact her husband. She explained the urgent situation to him and said she would meet him at the hospital. Roy told her to stay at home; he would go to the hospital and keep her posted. When he arrived, the emergency room doctor told him that his 19-month old baby girl probably would *not* live. She had suffered a massive brain hemorrhage—a stroke. Roy turned away with tears in his eyes. Later, Chelby was care-flighted to the hospital with a pediatric intensive care unit.

For the first time, we learned that Chelby was born with an arteriovenous malformation (AVM) of the brain. After doing some research on the Internet and after many discussions with various doctors, we all realized that a ruptured AVM is a very serious condition. A cerebral arteriovenous malformation is an abnormal connection between the arteries and veins in the brain that usually forms before birth and can vary in size and location in the brain. Basically, it is a mass of abnormal blood vessels which grow in the brain.

Cerebral AVMs occur in less than 1% of people and the cause is unknown. Although the condition is usually present at birth, symptoms such as severe headaches, seizures, paralysis or loss of coordination may occur at any age. Hemorrhages occur most often in people ages 15-20, but can also occur later in life. Some patients with an AVM also have cerebral aneurysms. There are three methods of treatment: (1) surgery, (2) radio surgery (i.e. radiation), and (3) embolization.

Chelby's case was rare, partly because it manifested itself in a baby. The AVM was extremely large and too deep in her brain for surgery to be considered a viable option. Also due to her age, embolization was ruled out as well. At this critical state, our only option was to keep her highly sedated and wait to see how her body responds to the trauma. The massive bleeding in Chelby's brain caused various complications, including the rising pressure in her brain. The attending surgeon at Medical City Dallas Children's Hospital asked permission to drill a hole in her head to relieve pressure.

Many friends, family and church members gathered in the lobby of the hospital to pray for our baby girl. After the procedure was completed, the doctor told us there was so much pressure on Chelby's brain you could literally hear the air coming out of her head. She needed extensive medical testing and other treatments as well, but the doctors decided to wait and give our precious baby time to heal before moving forward. She remained sedated and asleep for two weeks.

During this time, we were not allowed to hold Chelby. We also needed to keep our voices low as to not excite her and cause further complications.

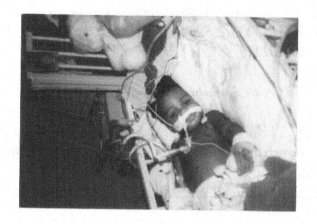

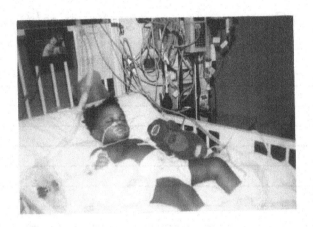

Inspirational Nugget Of Gold—Lesson #3
Created by the guidance of the Holy Spirit!

    Even though a situation may look bad and seem as though there is no hope. Remember, it's not over until God says it's over. The attending doctor said she probably would not live. ***Death and life are in the power of the tongue. Proverbs 18:21*** *Watch what you say. Speak it into* *your life and it becomes reality. Speak what you want not what you don't want.* **WHAT ARE YOU SAYING TO YOURSELF MENTALLY AND/OR AUDIBLY?**

Create something new and different.

P.S. In the space below, create your own nugget(s) of gold to inspire you to stay centered in the spirit of . . . **SPEAK POWER IN TO YOUR LIFE!**

Create your own nugget(s) of gold

_____

_____

_____

_____

_____

_____

_____

_____

_____

_____

_____

_____

_____

Chapter 4

My Talk with God

While in the emergency room, after Chelby's first stroke, I stood at the foot of her bed with my arms folded. I stared at my little 19-month old grandbaby's slightly twisted mouth, as she lay in a coma-like state. Inwardly, I asked a question: "God, did you give Chelby to us for a short period of time and now you are going to bring her back to you?"

I did not realize that one of the nurses in the emergency room was watching me. She said to me: "You can talk to her; she can hear you, even though she's asleep." I walked over to the left side of the table and took her hand in mine. I leaned over and whispered in her ear:

> *Chelby, you are a strong, powerful, baby girl of the Lord. I don't believe it is time for you to die. I think you are talking to the angels and playing with them right now. And I believe you have a testimony. So, come on back to us Chelby. You have a story to tell.*

Immediately, Chelby squeezed my hand tightly two times and instantaneously sat straight up. Her eyes were red and they opened very wide. I felt she was in great pain and very much afraid. She became nauseous, as doctors and nurses begin to rush over to the bed. Just as fast as she sat up, Chelby closed her eyes. She lay down and went back into a comma-like state.

I screamed: *Satan, you can't have her!* Then, I heard a voice say: **"She shall live and not die."** I felt the Spirit of the living God giving me strength and hope.

I know one day we will all die, but this was _not_ Chelby's time to leave us. The hospital Chaplain walked over to me and said, "I saw you transform at her bedside."

It was only because of my personal relationship with the Lord Jesus Christ that I could (while in shock and hurting) calmly walk over to Chelby's bedside and speak life to her. When you have this relationship and know who you are (in any situation) the spirit of the Almighty God that lives on the inside of you can take over; when you allow it to. I didn't have to think of what to say; it came naturally because of my continuous reading, studying, meditating and applying the WORD of God.

Inspirational Nugget Of Gold—Lesson #4
Created by the guidance of the Holy Spirit!

When we make a decision to develop a relationship with the Lord God by receiving Jesus (Yeshua—*Hebrew*) as our Lord and Savior, we can simply have a conversation with Him. He died for our sins, was buried, rose from the dead, walked this earth, ascended into heaven, and is sitting on the right hand side of the one and only living God. But He did not leave us comfortless; He left us a comforter, who is the Holy Spirit. The Holy Spirit guides, directs and instructs us in all things, if we seek Him. Understand, once you make this decision you are **NEVER** alone. If you want this awesome relationship, follow the steps listed below.

Receiving Christ is as simple as ABC

ADMIT—that you are a sinner.

> *Romans 3:23 All have sinned and come short of the glory of God.*

BELIEVE—that Jesus Christ died for you.
> *John 1:12 But as many as received Him, to them He gave the right to become children of God, to those who believe in His name:*

CONFESS—that Jesus Christ is Lord of your life.
> *Roman 10:9-10 If you confess with your mouth the Lord Jesus and believe in your heart that God has raised Him from the dead, you will be saved. For with the heart one believes unto righteousness, and with the mouth confession is made unto salvation.*

THEN PRAY THIS PRAYER:
Dear Lord Jesus, I know that I am a sinner. I believe that you died for my sins and rose from the grave. I now turn from my sins and invite you to come into my heart and life. I receive you as my personal Savior and follow you as my Lord. Amen REJOICE (from "The ABCs of Evangelism" *by Stan Toler***)**

> *Create something new and different.*

P.S. In the space below, simply write about the decision you have made in your own words . . . . ***THIS WILL BE THE MOST IMPORTANT DECISION OF YOUR LIFE!***

Create your own nugget(s) of gold

_____
_____
_____
_____
_____
_____
_____
_____
_____
_____
_____
_____
_____
_____
_____
_____
_____
_____
_____

Chapter 5

We Don't Need Sympathy

I remember friends and co-workers feeling very sorry for my family and me. They thought we were in denial about Chelby's condition. I told them: *if you don't just believe, and know that God will do what He said, please don't come to the hospital. We don't need sympathy. We need people with great faith!*

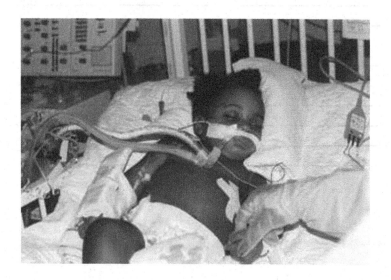

Chelby was asleep for about two weeks. During that time we played one song and sang it to her day and night, "Jesus Loves Me". One morning, my daughter and I were sitting next to her bed in the Intensive Care Unit of the hospital. Chijuana said, "Mama, I believe Chelby opened her eyes." We looked again and truly they were open.

We called for the nurse, who called for the doctor. She rushed over and examined her. But we noticed that Chelby would not look up at her. She just looked down. We asked, "Why is she looking downward?"

The doctor told us he had to give her morphine to keep her sleeping, because of the drains in her head. She was like a drug addict. When the drug was slowly stopped, eventually it wore off. After a few months in the hospital, thankfully, Chelby was able to go home.

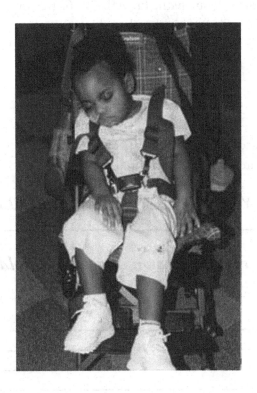

Often times, when there is traumatic situations in our lives, some individuals may begin (because of all the love that they have for us) to feel sorry. They may look at our tears while they strive to comfort us and the shocked looks on our faces, possibly thinking there is no faith. Not necessarily so. After we go through the immediate pain, we look up, get up and speak to that mountain. According to the scripture in Matthew 21:21, its got to move; and that's what we did.

Inspirational Nugget Of Gold—Lesson #5
Created by the guidance of the Holy Spirit!

When you are going through a bankruptcy, a disagreement with a close friend, or break-up of a relationship, or a loss of income, you don't need sympathy. Just trust in the Lord with all your heart, and lean not to your own understanding; in all your ways acknowledge him and He shall direct your path. Proverb 3:5-6. Remember, where two agree on anything, it is theirs for the asking. Matthew 18:19 Seek the friendship of an individual who will believe with you. Don't doubt, but trust, keep the faith and watch the Lord work.

Create something new and different.

P.S. In the space below, create your own nugget(s) of gold to inspire you to stay centered in the spirit of . . .

WHEN YOU ASK, BELIEVE AND RECEIVE IT!

Create your own nugget(s) of gold

_____

_____

_____

_____

_____

_____

_____

_____

_____

_____

_____

_____

_____

_____

_____

_____

_____

_____

_____

_____

Chapter 6

Challenge, After Challenge, After Challenge!

The first stroke in January dealt a huge devastating blow to our family. But there was yet more to come. We were truly challenged to our core.

When she was 23-months old, (May 2003) Chelby suffered a second stroke which was massive, while visiting family in Louisiana. After arriving at Our Lady of the Lake emergency room, doctors told my daughter and her husband to contact the next of kin; Chelby was not going to make it. Roy said: "they don't know what they are talking about." I was in the waiting room with the rest of my family. Everyone was sad. I asked them a question: ***Whose report shall we believe?*** Everyone shouted: "We shall believe the report of the Lord." Then I said, ***ok, let's be encouraged.***

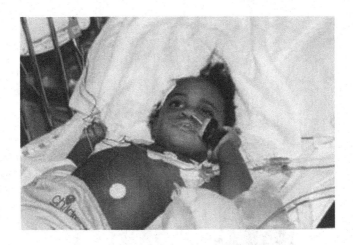

The hospital's chaplain came and guided me into a room where the doctor said Chelby was supposed to be dying. The chaplain proceeded to say: "I feel so sorry for this young couple." I asked: Why? He said: "Because their daughter is dying." I said: ***No, she is not dying. God said to me: "She shall live and not die."*** He looked at me very strangely. When I saw Chelby, she was again in a comma-like state. I told the doctor: ***I don't see death. I see life.*** I truly did <u>not</u> see death. She looked like she was just sleeping. The doctor also looked at me in a strange way.

They begin to move Chelby to a room in the Intensive Care Unit. Only two people at a time could stay in the room with her, so her great-grandmother and I accompanied Chelby. As the attendants were rolling her bed, Chelby's left arm went straight in the air. Her left leg did the same thing. Her great grandmother said: "Bren, look!" I said: I know Mama. God is only confirming for me what he promised: ***"she shall live and not die."***

In June 2003, she was transported by air to Children's Medical City in Dallas and underwent surgery to clip the aneurysm and remove a portion of the AVM. In July 2003, a shunt was placed in her brain to help her body process cerebral spinal fluid. Chelby was hospitalized until October 2003.

Her right side was weak and her vision was affected due to the strokes. At that time, doctors said that Chelby might never regain her vision. Chelby received physical therapy, occupational therapy, vision therapy and various other therapies.

All and all, this has been an extremely emotional and traumatic ordeal. At times, we felt as if we wanted to give up. But, we could not give up because Chelby refused to give up. Today, she continues to fight. She just won't stop!

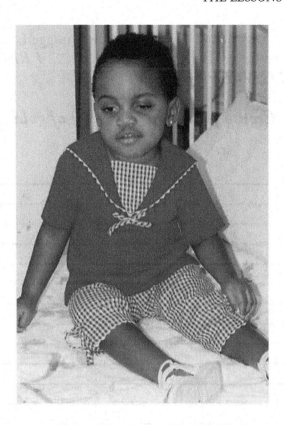

Inspirational Nugget of Gold—Lesson #6
Created by the guidance of the Holy Spirit!

Philippians 4:13, "I can do all things through Christ who strengthens me. Henry Ford said, "If you think you can do it, or if you think you can't do it, you are right." Don't ever use the word "can't" again. When that word shows up in your spirit, think about the little engine who can; know that's "YOU".

Create something new and different.

P.S. In the space below, create your own nugget(s) of gold to inspire you to stay centered in the spirit of . . . *I REFUSE TO QUIT OR GIVEUP!*

Create your own nugget(s) of gold

_____

_____

_____

_____

_____

_____

_____

_____

_____

_____

_____

_____

_____

_____

_____

_____

_____

_____

_____

_____

Chapter 7

The Warrior in Chelby

Three years later in October of 2006, Chelby suffered a third stroke. After this stroke and her stay in the hospital, people came to visit in hopes of encouraging the family. Sometimes Chelby would surprise them by asking: *"Can I pray for you?"* Then, she would pray a one-sentence prayer by saying: *"God please heal them and make them feel better."* Some would leave with tears in their eyes.

Sometimes, Chelby would ask: *"Can I sing a song for you?"* When a visitor said yes, she would sing the song "Jesus Loves Me." We never taught her this song, even though we played it in the hospital day, after day, after day.

Chelby would also sing another song entitled "Praise Is What I Do." She would say: *"It's what I do; it's what I do; it's what I do!"* She repeated this part of the song over and over. All were amazed at Chelby's courage and her strength. Tears were very common back then.

Chelby is now 8 years old and continues to live with the ramifications of three strokes and a shunt in her brain. Her challenges have _not_ stopped and Chelby has _not_ stopped either. You see, Chelby is a fighter . . . a warrior, whose strength and perseverance we admire and benefit from enormously.

She can see, walk and talk. Doctors are amazed at her progress because the area in the brain, where her motor skills are located, was damaged. She has been diagnosed as totally disabled and totally blind. Doctors have not been able to operate again on Chelby because opening up her skull may cause her to become a vegetable.

We live each day in faith believing what the Spirit of God spoke to me at the time of Chelby's first stroke in Baylor Hospital: ***"She shall live and not die."*** You see, this experience is about Chelby, but it is really <u>*not*</u> for her.

I believe with all my heart that the purpose of Chelby's experience is to encourage me, my family and many others who may be going through an illness or some other serious life challenge. Her story helps us all understand that . . . ***we must never give up!***

Inspirational Nugget Of Gold—Lesson #7
Created by the guidance writ!

There are times in our lives we just need to know that someone loves us. Sometimes parents are there, sons and daughters are there, husbands, wives, friends, and co-workers are there, but there still seems to be something missing. It is not until we realize the only one that can fill that void is the Son of the living God, Jesus. Then, we can see how Chelby's favorite song heals our broken and lonely hearts. She sings, "Jesus Love Me This I know; For the Bible tells me so. Little ones to Him belong, they are weak but He is strong. Yes, Jesus loves me; yes, Jesus loves me; yes, Jesus loves me for the Bible tells me so." When we understand that He really does love us unconditionally, there is great joy and amazing peace that overtake us.

Create something new and different.

P.S. In the space below, create your own nugget(s) of gold to inspire you to stay centered in the spirit of . . . ***THERE IS NONE LIKE HIM!***

Create your own nugget(s) of gold

Chapter 8

Confident, Even When Trouble is Near

During January and March 2010, Chelby experienced a fourth major seizure and stroke, respectively. Doctors did not know what to do about the activities that were occurring in her brain. The plan was to meet in two months and they would make recommendations that might help Chelby.

Chelby experienced the fourth seizure at school. It was a major one! Her eyes rolled back and she had serious shakes. Upon returning home, Chelby was a little weak, but again walking, talking, singing as normal. There were several doctor appointments scheduled that forced her mother to take off from work without pay to handle all of them.

The first day her mom was off from work, the day care Assistant Director called and said that Chelby was vomiting and she was very sleepy. Because Chijuana was off from work, she was able to get to Chelby's day care in five minutes. She was able to get Chelby to Children's Hospital in less than an hour.

Chelby actually walked into the hospital while having the stroke. She eventually went to sleep and it appeared that the doctors prepared for the worst. There were numerous tubes in her mouth and her nostril. As we waited for the test results, Chelby's godparents came to see her in the intensive care unit.

The nurse told us that we could talk to her because she can hear us. We told Chelby how special she is to God. "***God loves you and all is well***"; *we whispered in her ears.*

Hours later, the hospital staff removed all tubes. Immediately after that Chelby woke up and recognized us. She said, "Hi daddy; hi mommy; hi LaLa." We all smiled and said: "look at God!"

But there was still something wrong. After more tests, doctors said there was a possible problem with the shunt in her brain. They may have to repair it. After receiving all the test results and discussing this with one another, we had to do what we believed was best for Chelby. The decision was made to pursue another operation. Once inside Chelby's brain, they found that the shunt was fine. Next, they checked the tube attached to the shunt and found that it was blocked. After replacing the tube, Chelby was left with 10 staples in the front of her head and 10 in a large area in the back of her head.

The next day the nurse wanted Chelby to potty in a pull-up because she thought Chelby was too weak to get up. Chelby said: "No, that's nasty." She wanted to use the pot. We all laughed and the nurse helped Chelby out of the bed to use the pot. On the third day, Chelby was walking up and down the halls of the hospital singing "Jesus Loves Me." Again, the nurses, doctors and others were amazed at her speedy recovery. She remained there a few days just to make sure all was well.

One evening, while I was sitting in the hospital with Chelby she said, "LaLa." I said: yes, Chelby. She said to me, "I am so grateful." I said: so am I, Chelby. Then, I thought *WOW*; this little 8-year old baby girl truly is amazing!

Later, my daughter asked Chelby: "Are you happy?" Immediately, Chelby came back with: "Yes, what about you?" That statement blew my daughter away!

We are confident that God's hand continues to guide Chelby. He brings her back stronger than ever, after all the seizures, strokes, aneurisms, and shunt.

I remember, approximately one week prior to Chelby's fourth stroke, she chanted over and over and over: "***He's an awesome God! He's an awesome God! He's an awesome God!***" My pastor said, as I mentioned Chelby's actions to him: "God talks to

Chelby; in her chanting, she was building herself up, because she knew in her spirit trouble was on the horizon." ***What better way to build herself up, than through lifting up the name of the Most High God?***

Inspirational Nugget Of Gold—Lesson #8
Created by the guidance of the Holy Spirit!

When you know—that you know—that you know, all is well, nothing can stop you from succeeding; not even trouble. You **MUST** have complete confidence in knowing that you can **NEVER** lose with the Lord by your side. Matt 28:20 Therefore, when challenges move toward you, and they will, (know that it's just a part of life's test and becoming more mature) have confidence in knowing that the presence of God is with you and say, "OK, let's take this mountain!" How do you take the mountain? With your words; speak to it to be gone, trust, have faith, don't doubt, be patient and stand. **I KNOW I'M RIGHT!** Chelby's chanting was her speaking to the mountain because the awesome God stepped in on her behalf as He will do for you. He is no respecter of persons.

Create something new and different.

P.S. In the space below, create your own golden nugget(s) to inspire you to stay centered in the spirit of . . . ***SPEAK TO THE MOUNTAIN!***

Create your own golden nugget(s)

_____
_____
_____
_____
_____
_____
_____
_____
_____
_____
_____
_____
_____
_____
_____
_____
_____
_____
_____
_____

Chapter 9

The Decision

Two months passed by quickly. It was time for Roy and Chijuana to meet with Chelby's surgeon. As they walked in his office, they could tell that the news was not good, nor encouraging. He gave them two choices.

The first choice was to perform another surgery called Hemespherectomy. This meant removing half the brain; the portion of Chelby's brain that has caused the bleedings since 2003. The doctor explained that this choice comes with **NO** guarantees. Chelby could become a vegetable and **never** regain consciousness. She may not have **ANY** quality of life, she would just exist. **The second choice** was to do nothing and she would continue to have strokes and/or seizures until one causes her death. Quite naturally, Roy and Chijuana had tears in their eyes, after receiving this information.

As they had prayed for direction from God, they discussed the two choices. Their decision was _**not**_ to have another surgery. Instead, they would continue to trust God for their daughter's healing. On the other side of that decision, they also realized that God could bring Chelby home to be with Him. So, they contacted the immediate family members to inform them of their decision. Chijuana especially wanted everyone to know that should Chelby go home to be with God, she did not want any questioning of their decision.

We are all believers in Jesus Christ and trust God's perfect will to be done. Everyone is at peace, knowing that Chelby is in the **BEST** hands, the hands of God.

We will continue to live each day to its fullest with her and know that all is well. Who knows, Chelby may out live all of us. We have done what the Bible says: "Make your request known to the Father". All IS WELL!

Inspirational Nugget Of Gold—Lesson #9
Created by the guidance of the Holy Spirit!

Perhaps, over the years you have been taught that whatever life brings, especially if it's bad, that this must be the will of God because he allowed it to happen. Therefore, you must accept it. THE DEVIL IS A LIAR! God is good, God is good, God is good. He sent His son that you might have life and have it more abundantly. Remember, when you read, study, mediate, and apply the word of God to **YOUR** life, **NOTHING IS IMPOSSIBLE!**

Create something new and different.

P.S. In the space below, create your own golden nugget(s) to inspire you to stay centered in the spirit of . . .

MAKE A DECISION! CHOOSE TO BE HAPPY!

Create your own golden nugget(s)

_____

_____

_____

_____

_____

_____
_____
_____
_____
_____
_____
_____
_____
_____
_____
_____
_____
_____
_____
_____

Chapter 10

A New Beginning

Thus far, doctors can't really do anything more for Chelby to help her completely heal. Nevertheless, each day of our lives we walk in faith believing that all is well!

Today, Chelby continues to persevere. I love it! She can't lose with what she uses. Every day there is more power in her words. You see, we have taught Chelby that she is strong and that she can do anything she wants. Almost daily, Chelby says: *"I can do all things through Christ who strengthen me." Phil 4:13*

I can walk.
I can talk.
I can see.
I can read.
I can write.
I'm strong.
I'm a miracle.
I'm a testimony, in Jesus' name.
Amen, Amen, Amen.
Hallelujah!
Praise the Lord!
Glory!

Inspirational Golden Nugget—Lesson #10
Created by the guidance of the Holy Spirit!

It is sooo important to speak what you want and not what you don't want. Think about all the things you have to be grateful for in your own life right now. If you can't think of anything because you are going through a challenging time let me help you. Thank you Father God for waking me up this morning, for the air that I breath, for another opportunity to live this day to its fullest, for your love, peace, hope, faith, joy, grace and mercy . . . . Maybe you are thinking that you don't have all of these, but you do have some. Keep thinking and I am sure others will come to mind. We know these things now, say it like Chelby, "I can make it, I'm not alone, it's possible, I'm living my best life today, I am debt free and on, and on, and on.

Create something new and different.

P.S. In the space below, create your own golden nugget(s) to inspire you to stay centered in the spirit of . . . *I CAN DO WHAT I PUT MY MIND TO DO!*

_____

Create your own golden nugget(s)

_____
_____
_____
_____
_____
_____
_____
_____
_____

_____
_____
_____
_____
_____
_____
_____
_____
_____
_____

Chapter 11

My <u>AH-HA</u> Moment

As I stated earlier in this story, these lessons may be about Chelby, but they are *<u>not</u>* for Chelby. They are for those of us who are challenged today. Life and death are in the power of our tongue. What we say has great value, great power, and it can affect what happens in our lives. Some famous quotes remind me of this simple truth:

> *"If you think you can or if you think you can't, both are right."*—**Henry Ford**

> *"When life experiences knock you down, strive to land on your back, because if you can look up, you can get up!"*—**Les Brown**

When my daughter called me and said that Chelby had a fourth stroke, I had a little talk with God in the name of Jesus!

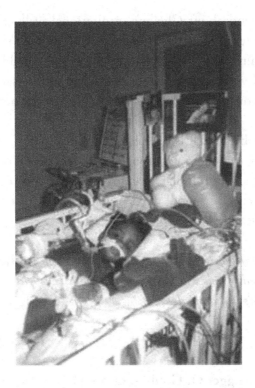

I asked Him: Lord, what is it? Is it something that I need to do? Is there something that my daughter and her husband need to do? What is it Lord? What is it?

God said to me: "It's not Chelby. I got Chelby. It's you and your family." My reply was: What Lord? He said: "You have lost your joy. I know that you believe in me. I know that you love me. I know that you have a relationship with me, but you have lost your joy. Because of life's challenges and life's ups and down, you have lost your joy."

Then He said: "It's *not* just you and your family, but Christians in general. This message is *not* for lost souls, but for those who say that they believe in me. I want you to give this message to every Christian that I allow you to speak with."

Of course, I said: Yes Lord! I was in awe; as I listened to the Spirit of the Lord speak to my inner person.

As I have been sharing this message from God with others, it has been amazing what has transpired. For example, when I told my

85-year-old friend about Chelby's inspirational walk in life, she just broke down in tears. She said, "I knew something wasn't right with me; I knew something was wrong." She agreed that she had lost her joy.

I've shared with a male friend in Atlanta and he said: "you know what Brenda, you're right!" I shared with a business owner and associate of mine and she welled up in tears also. She said, "You must tell it and write the book Brenda. It is so needed."

I've shared that message from God with many others and the responses were all very similar. Even, sharing with one of my aunts, all she could say was, "MY God!" This was and is my exact sentiment! My decision was clear:

> *I am __not__ going to live my life without the joy God has provided for us and I will __not__ leave this world without joy! This is a done deal for me.*

Inspirational Nugget Of Gold—Lesson #11
Created by the guidance of the Holy Spirit!

Sometimes in life, we just don't get it or it takes time for us to get it. Our Ah-Ha moment is when it finally clicks for us, which is different for all of us. One day while reading, mediating, praying, dancing, singing, conversing, or just being quiet, it happens. That moment when a solution to a problem becomes crystal clear, the point where you are trying to figure something out or understand why this is happening or may be after a very challenging situation in life occurs and you may be wondering what's next. In a still quiet moment like a bolt of lightning, it hits you. There it is . . . your answer, solution, direction, and understanding followed by sweet, sweet peace. Now, you know the why, what, when and how. Oh my God, what peace, what joy, what hope and **WHAT A NEW LIFE!** OK, it's your turn. Write it down.

Create something new and different.

P.S. In the space below, create your own golden nugget(s) to inspire you to stay centered in the spirit of . . .

IN ALL YOUR GETTING GET UNDERSTANDING!

Create your own golden nugget(s)

_____

_____

_____

_____

_____

_____

_____

_____

_____

_____

_____

_____

_____

_____

_____

_____

Chapter 12

She Shall Live and Not Die

The doctors have spoken and there is nothing else that they can do. So, we said to ourselves, "we suppose this is it as far as the doctors are concerned." What do we do? We continue to pray, have faith, wait on the Lord, and expect Chelby's healing." Then, oh my God, Chelby experienced a fifth stroke. The surgeon decides that something must be done. For seven years we were told that the AVM was inoperable. Now, we are told it must be done in order to save Chelby's life. I believe it was an answer to our prayers when Dr. Swift said, "Chelby is special to me. I am going after the largest AVM. This will be a major brain surgery; one that has never been done before. Because Chelby's situation is very unique, the surgeon was somewhat nervous and the parents were extremely uneasy, and concerned, but hopeful, God would do what's best for our baby girl Chelby. Let me set the stage for you. We knew this was warfare; we positioned ourselves for battle. We begin sharing with prayer warriors locally and throughout the country; who in turn informed their church members, prayer groups and other prayer warriors. The Youth Leader from my church, Light Church, challenged youth and other members to unite in fasting and praying; saying the same thing by reading scriptures on health and healing from the church's confession book. We fasted from 6:00 pm on the day prior to Chelby's surgery until 6:00 pm on the day of surgery. For nine hours we sat and waited with great confidence. Periodically, we would get an update from the surgeon that everything was going well. Finally, Dr. Swift came out with a huge smile on his face. Roy said, "Is she moving?" He said, "She moved her left leg. I asked, "Can she talk?" He said,

"She has a tube in her throat, but you can see her in about an hour." After an hour, we walked in recovery and as we entered, we could hear Chelby crying, "My ear, my ear, my ear." We have never been so glad to hear her in pain. We just praised God. Chelby was awake, crying and moving. Hallelujah!!! After the visitors left and her parents went home to shower and rest a bit, I was left alone with Chelby. I got close to her face and said, "Chelby, do you know who I am?" She said, "Yes, Brenda Parker." Oh my God, I was so excited. Then, she asked the nurse to give her water with ice, her Barney DVD and her black purse. We all just laughed. One of the nurses, who had never worked with Chelby before said, "Wow, this little girl is strong. The nurse who had worked with Chelby previously said, "Oh, that's Chelby". She knew the strength in her. Within three days, Chelby was walking to the potty and singing. Three days after being released, Chelby was climbing sixteen stairs. What a miracle! Our God truly is an awesome God.

It has been about two months. Chelby is being home schooled and doing very well. Her pediatrician has released her to return to school. We are waiting for a follow-up visit with her neurosurgeon, which includes an angiogram. This will reveal what remains in her brain or if there is a need for another Gamma Knife (radiation) treatment. We know that all is well because God has said, **"SHE SHALL LIVE AND NOT DIE and declare the works of the Lord"**.

Chelby continues to live life to its fullest as though nothing has taken place. I love her spirit and the confidence to live with no concern about life's challenges. It's as though she is saying NEXT. What about you?

Inspirational Nugget Of Gold—Lesson #12
Created by the guidance of the Holy Spirit!

No matter what happens in your life, you shall live and not die. Life will deal you a lemon sometimes, it will issue challenges, and it will cause heart breaks, as well as life threatening situations, but it is not over until GOD says it is over. Remember this, "You are the head and not the tail, you are above and not beneath, you are the lender and not the borrower, you are blessed and not cursed." *(Duet 28)* Know these things, speak them, meditate on them, apply them, walk in this, and make it your life. It truly is who you are. Like Chelby, know that you know that you know that you know, God has created you to win in every area of your life. SO, GO GET YOUR STUFF! That is the promises of GOD.

Create something new and different.

P.S. In the space below, create your own golden nugget(s) to inspire you to stay centered in the spirit of . . .

LEARN THE PROMISES AND GET WHAT'S YOURS!

Create your own golden nugget(s)

_____

_____

_____

_____

_____

_____

_____

_____

_____

_____

_____

_____
_____
_____
_____
_____
_____
_____
_____

Chapter 13

Our "Warrior Princess"

(From The Parent's Perspective)

On the morning of Chelby's last surgery, a very dear friend in Houston sent me a text message saying, " . . . . Praying for your Warrior Princess." As I began to reflect on the last ten years, I thought "WOW" what an awesome description of our little princess. Chelby is truly a warrior; she has been fighting for her life since before she was born. Shortly after Roy and I found out we were expecting, I began to have complications and had to go to the hospital. In the Emergency Room I was told that I could potentially loose our baby. The next few months went by without incident. I began to gain weight, the baby was developing normally and we learned we were having a baby girl. Then, at 29 weeks I went into premature labor! My water broke, I developed pneumonia, was hospitalized and placed on strict bed rest. This meant being confined to the bed . . . 24 hours a day . . . for everything including bathing and bathroom duty! I was both scared and embarrassed. I was literally in bed for everything. When the technicians came in to change the bed linens, I had to roll over on my side. When I needed to bathe, I had to settle for a wipe off in the bed. Then, there was the bed pan when I needed to go to the bathroom. I could get on and off of the bed pan without assistance. I mastered that technique very quickly. Of course someone had to empty the bed pan and I was too embarrassed to call the nurses' station for assistance. I would wait for my mother or Roy to visit. Then, they would try to determine who was last to empty my bed pan. Roy would say to my mother 'It's your turn' and she would say 'No, I think it's your turn'. They really got a kick out of my situation. This was possibly the most humiliating experience of my life.

I was only allowed out of the bed for sonograms which included being transported in a wheel chair. The doctors were very concerned about the possibility of me delivering so early. If she were born at that time, Chelby would have serious complications including undeveloped lungs and potential blindness. The worst case scenario was that she wouldn't survive. We were terrified! All of my life I thought . . . when your water breaks, the baby is born. I didn't realize it was possible to hold a baby for any additional time. My focus changed when the doctor explained I was literally a human incubator. I was growing a baby and we needed to buy as much time as possible. I needed to eat properly, get lots of rest and remain stress free in order to deliver a healthy baby girl. After three long and uncomfortable weeks, Chelby was born at 32 weeks. She weighed 3 pounds, 13.8 ounces. She was so tiny; Roy could hold her in one hand.

Premature babies are usually required to remain hospitalized until their due date. This meant I would go home and Chelby would remain in the hospital for eight more weeks. It was a very heart wrenching experience to leave the hospital without my baby. Yet, I was still grateful because at least I had a baby. Somewhere in the world there was a mother that would go home without her baby and God allowed our baby into the world. Although this was a complicated situation, we continued to be thankful. Our God is such an awesome God . . . to our surprise; Chelby was discharged after only three weeks!!! This was just the beginning of the manifestation of Chelby's fighting spirit!

After being discharged, Chelby continued to thrive to live. She met all milestones such as crawling and babbling like any full term baby. She even took her first steps just two days after her first birthday. Life was good and our baby was 'normal', without any complications, so we thought.

By the fall of 2002, we were expecting our third daughter and I found myself on bed rest again. Although I was hospitalized, I was allowed out of my bed. I was so excited. I could shower, sit in the rocking chair and even handle my own bathroom duty. My family would visit and Chelby would climb in the bed with me. I really wanted to go home so I began to plead with my doctor to set me free (I can be a little dramatic). I promised to be the best patient if allowed to go home. I would remain on bed rest. I guess the pleading worked because I was finally discharged three days before Christmas. Chelby had the best Christmas ever. She was so excited with all of her toys and gifts. Her favorites were a keyboard and chicken dance Elmo. I will never forget the expression on her face that Christmas morning. It was pure bliss.

Every day Chelby would climb in bed with me and Roy would prepare peanut butter and jelly sandwiches for us. We truly enjoyed our time together. After a few weeks at home, I began to cry during our time together. I was overwhelmed with emotions and would ask God to protect my baby girl. I prayed a hedge of protection around her, I asked God to keep her from all harm and danger. I just cried and prayed. I didn't tell anyone of my experiences. I attributed the emotions to my hormones. Then, the cold day in January . . . .

Chelby's first stroke left me devastated and confused. I couldn't understand why God was allowing this to happen to my precious baby girl. Although Chelby's left side was weakened by the stroke, she recovered quickly. Since she couldn't walk, my mother taught her to pull herself around on the floor and my brother taught her to maneuver the staircase. By April, Chelby was walking and talking again. We were learning to cope with the changes to our baby girl.

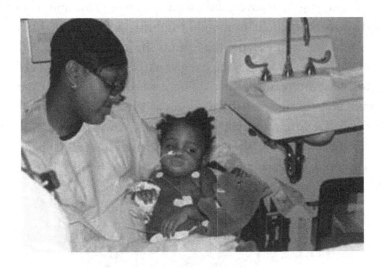

After the second stroke, I was angry; angry with the world, angry when I saw 'normal' children, angry because I felt my child wasn't given an opportunity to be 'normal'. The second stroke erased all of the progress we experienced and also affected her eyesight. We would wave our hand in front of Chelby's face and she wouldn't notice. I began to question why God would allow this to happen again. I questioned why God would allow us to have another baby; if we were going to have a special needs baby that required so much attention. I couldn't understand how I could care for both babies nor did I have the strength to endure. To make matters even worse, Roy and I were both laid off. It was a difficult time for our family. We had a teenage daughter in high school, a baby in the intensive care unit and a new born baby to also take care of. I wanted to give up.

During the next several years I realized several things. My daughter may not have been what society labeled as normal, but she was different. She was a *fighter* from the beginning. No matter what happened to Chelby, she would continue to fight. Things that would cause an average person to quit, she would continue to press on. Through all of the surgeries, needles, procedures and examinations, she would fight. We would try to keep her calm, but she would continue to fight. One day we were sitting in recovery following an angiogram and a nurse explained to us the benefit of a child's fighting spirit. She said "you always want her to fight because that means she hasn't given up. When she stops fighting and resisting, she has given up. At that point of giving up, she will have no reason to live." Those words spoke to my soul. I could never give up on my baby! As long as she continues to fight, I have to FIGHT. No matter how difficult our circumstances were, no matter how many times we were laid off, no matter how much pain we were in, we could not give up. We must continue to fight!

By the third stroke, I was different. I no longer had a defeated or helpless attitude. I had learned how to not only manage the pain and disappointments, but God has given me the strength to endure. I refused to allow the enemy to steal my joy; He could not have my baby!!!! I'm not saying that I don't get emotional or weak at times, I'm grateful for God's grace and mercy. Over the course of Chelby's experiences, I've met many families facing similar or worse conditions. When you think that your situation is unbearable, you meet someone else whose situation is much worse than your own.

One day as I was waiting for Chelby to complete her physical and occupational therapy, I exchanged stories with several mothers in the waiting area at Children's Medical Center. At this point, I was still in the 'woe is me' phase. One mother looked at me and said "I wish I were in your shoes. You have one thing I will never experience. I will never hear my daughter call me mommy or say I love you. She will never speak. Even though you have your challenges, your daughter can call you mommy and say I love you". I will always cherish those words. I don't remember her name or face, but we are forever connected by those words.

Even though Chelby has experienced a total of five strokes, several seizures, two shunt revisions, multiple procedures and two brain surgeries, God continues to keep her. She is a happy girl; probably the happiest person I know. She has a sparkling personality and an infectious laugh. She touches the hearts of all who know her and anyone she meets. I have learned so much from watching her as she grows. A dear friend called Chelby the 'Ultimate Excuse Buster'.

Inspirational Nugget of Gold—Lesson #13
Created by the guidance of the Holy Spirit!

What is the "Ultimate Excuse Buster"? It's when you've gone through various trials and tribulations and you think you can't make it. There are no excuses, when you read about Chelby Cymone Terrell. She walked through the storm, the valley and the deepest sea, but in the end the "Ultimate Excuse Buster" danced in the rain. How about you? What's your next move? Will you dance with Chelby no matter what the challenge might be?

Create something new and different.

P.S. In the space below, create your own golden nugget(s) to inspire you to stay centered in the spirit of . . . *THE ULTIMATE EXCUSE BUSTER!*

Create your own golden nugget(s)

_____

_____

_____

_____

_____

_____

_____

_____

_____

_____

_____

_____

_____

_____

_____

_____

_____

_____

_____

Chapter 14

Chelby My Chelby

(by Chelby's Oldest Sister Chantel)

Being an older sibling, especially when there is a significant age difference, gives a person a sense of responsibility. When my sisters were born I felt like they were my children. I wanted to feed them, dress them, and do everything for them and none of that has changed.

When Chelby had her first stroke, like most of my family, I was in shock. I had never had someone close to me be that sick so I did not know how to process what had happened. The hardest thing was seeing her in such a helpless state and not being able to help her. I always felt that I had to protect my sisters so to not be able to help Chelby was very difficult for me. My family, especially my grandmother, has always taught me about having my own personal relationship with God, so from an early age I knew how to make my requests known. So I did the only thing I knew how to do, I prayed from the bottom of my heart that God would heal my sister.

When Chelby came home after her first stroke, physical therapist, occupational therapist, and many other specialists came to the house to help her get back on her feet. I was even more overprotective of Chelby after she got sick so whenever I was home, I would sit in on her therapy sessions to see what they were doing and to ask questions. I grew very interested in her physical therapy sessions because they used to make Chelby most uncomfortable, so naturally I had many questions for her therapist. As time went on the type of questions I asked began to change. Initially I would ask what she was doing and why, but I began asking her what made her want to be a therapist and how long she had to go to school to be a therapist. After Chelby's second stroke and continued therapy, I decided to pursue a degree in Physical Therapy.

After I finished school, I no longer felt helpless because I was familiar with Chelby's illness and the treatment she was receiving so my role as the protective sister had been renewed. When Chelby had a doctor's appointment I sent my parents with a list of questions to ask or my mom would conference me in so I could hear what the doctor was saying and ask questions. Although, I could not make Chelby's illness go away or take away her pain I felt that I could help ease her pain and take better care of her. Although I relocated to Louisiana, whenever Chelby was sick or had a major procedure I was there, and when I couldn't be there Chelby would have my mom call me to sing her favorite song "Yes Jesus Loves Me." Throughout Chelby's journey I have tried to protect her, ease her pain when I could, and when I couldn't ease her pain I tried to make her as comfortable as I could.

When she woke up from her first stroke I read her favorite book, when she had her second shunt revision and her second brain surgery I cleaned her wounds and washed her hair when she wouldn't let anyone else do it, and throughout her journey when she needed comfort I would sing "Yes Jesus Loves Me."

My family has been told a number of times that Chelby wouldn't walk, talk, sing, dance, or do many of the things she does and for that I thank God! I also thank God for the entire therapist teams that helped her and they are still helping her with her physical disabilities today. I thank God for all of the various specialists that assisted Chelby during her challenges. I truly thank God for her surgeon, Dr. Swift and his family who loves Chelby as though she is their daughter. May the Lord richly bless you and keep you.

Inspirational Nugget of Gold—Lesson #14

Created by the guidance of the Holy Spirit!

Are there people in your life whom you have not appreciated as you should?

Of course, we know that they are not perfect and they like you and I sometimes make wrong choices and/or decisions. But, would the world be as great as it is without them. Show some love with a smile, a hug, a thank you or just with a pleasant look. Don't be hard and don't be shy! Go for it. You CAN do it.

Create something new and different.

P.S. In the space below, create your own golden nugget(s) to inspire you to stay centered in the spirit of . . . *LIFE'S TRIALS AND TESTS ARE THE EVENTS THAT 'EXERCISE' OUR FAITH MUSCLES.*

Create your own golden nugget(s)

_____

_____

_____

_____

_____

_____

_____

_____

_____

_____

_____

_____

_____

_____

_____

_____

_____

_____

_____

_____

Chapter 15

Our Father Will Be There When We Get There

When I look at Chelby and spend time with her, I realize experiencing joy is so easy when we know where our joy comes from. It starts with making a decision to agree with the WORD of God, believing: *"The joy of the Lord is my strength."*

I've come to realize that the only way to get back to it (JOY) or acquire it is to have a relationship with God's son Jesus. For me, I had to ask for forgiveness, since I let my joy go because of life challenges. I had to make a choice to take my joy back, as we all must do when life's troubles become so demanding and challenging.

Each day, I continue to learn from **"The Lessons of Chelby"**. I wake-up excited about life, because I know God has allowed me to live another day. Then I say as Chelby says with a big smile: "Is it wake-up time?" I start thanking God for another day and asking Him to guide me—like a fellow entrepreneur once said:

This day, dear God, go before me and touch every thing, every situation, every person before I get there.

Is that powerful? After I pray this prayer, no matter what I encounter during the day, I know God is already there!!! This means every day of my life my Father will be there when I get there. The same is true for all of YOU. Hallelujah!!!!!!!!!

I know that one day God will use Chelby to tell her story, or maybe even sing it. In the meantime, God has said to me: "Brenda, you are my ambassador to get this message to the world." I'm excited about this assignment and I'll be like Dr. Martin Luther King Jr.—a drum major for impacting people's lives, in the best way that I can.

Looking back on a 19-month old baby girl, who today is 10 years old, and has <u>not</u> stopped; She says: ***"Sometimes I've got to move it, move it, MO—VE IT!!!***

I know that's just a song Chelby learned at school, but how appropriate! She reminds us that no matter what our situation might be, it's possible to go through the storm with a dynamic, powerful, positive attitude of: ***"I think I can! I know I can make it!"***

Again, this story is for **YOU!** Is anything too hard for God—the **ONE** who created all things? I would say emphatically—**"NO."**

The scriptures provide us with some powerful reminders that work without a doubt, when we apply them. The Word of God states: "All things work together for the good of those who love the Lord and are called according to His purpose." *(Roman 8:28) No matter what things look like, remember they are working together for your good. Believe and don't doubt no matter what!* It also reminds us to: "Trust in the Lord with all our heart and lean not to our own understanding, in all our ways acknowledge Him and He shall direct your path. *(Proverb 3:5-6 paraphrased)*

Life is so very precious. You <u>can</u> live a complete, fulfilled life, and help someone else soar like an eagle. This book contains powerful principles and lessons that will lift you every time you have a need to be encouraged or when you just want to confirm that you're on track and moving in the right direction to claim your JOY.

Set goals. Know what you want and go get it. Be mindful that ***"Information Minus Application Equals Stagnation." (by Brenda A. Parker)*** If you don't apply the things that you learn, you will be spinning your wheels. If you keep on doing what you're doing, you will keep getting what you're normally getting. Keep moving while you practice, practice, practice *The Lessons of Chelby.* Use the lessons to change and enhance your life. Receive them in your heart from a little girl named Chelby Cymone Terrell, who wakes up in the morning with the same question—*"Is it wake-up time?"* Then with a smile, she's ready and eager to give the **WORLD** a hug and a kiss!

CHELBY TODAY

UNTIL WE MEET AGAIN

APPENDIX

APPENDIX

Chelby's Medical History

January 23, 2003 Suffered 1ˢᵗ stroke at 19 months old, diagnosed with AVM. Hospitalized for 3 weeks—Medical City Dallas Hospital

May 24, 2003 Suffered 2ⁿᵈ stroke—Hospitalized at Our Lady of the Lake Hospital—Baton Rouge, LA

June 2003 Transferred from Our Lady of the Lake to Children's Medical Center—Dallas Surgery—Craniotomy to clamp Aneurysm and remove Fistula

July 2003 Shunt Placement

September 2003 Transferred to Our Children's House at Baylor

November 2003 Discharged from Hospital—Our Children's House at Baylor

February 2004 Gamma Knife (radiation)

October 2006 Suffered 3ʳᵈ Stroke—Hospitalized 3 weeks at Children's Medical Center—Dallas
1ˢᵗ Shunt Revision

February 2007 Gamma Knife (radiation)

July 2009 Tendon Transfer

March 2010 Suffered 4ᵗʰ Stroke—Hospitalized at Children's Medical Center—Dallas

April 2010 2nd Shunt Revision

October 2010   Suffered 5th Stroke—Hospitalized at Children's
                        Medical Center—Dallas

November 2010   Surgery—Craniotomy to remove AVM

DAILY AFFIRMATIONS

(Read 3 times a day)

- I can do all things through Christ which strengthens me. *Phil. 4:13*

- But my God shall supply all my need according to His riches in glory by Christ Jesus. *Phil. 4:19*

- In all things I am more than a conqueror through Him that loves me. *Romans 8:37*

- If God be for me, who can be against me? *Roman 8:31b*

- Greater is He that is in me, than he that is in the world. *1 John 4:4*

- Death and life are in the power of my tongue. *Proverb 18:21a*

- Trust in the Lord with all your heart, and lean not to your own understanding, in all your ways acknowledge Him and He will direct your paths. *Proverbs 3:5-6*

- I will delight myself in the Lord and He will give me the desires of my heart. *Psalm 37:4*

- I will not be weary in well doing; for in due season I shall reap if I faint not. *Galatians 5:16*

- God will instruct me and teach me in the way I should go; He will guide me with His eye. *Psalm 32:8*

- Now unto Him that is able to do exceedingly abundantly above all that I ask or think, according to the power that works in me, unto Him be glory. *Ephesians 3:20*

ALWAYS REMEMBER

- For as he thinks in his heart, so is he. *Proverbs 23:7 (NKJ)*

- Have faith in God. *Mark 11:22b*

- "What the mind of man can conceive and believe, the mind of man can achieve" **Norman Vincent Peale**

- "Information Minus Application Equals Stagnation" *Brenda A. Parker*

- When you want what you've never had, you must do what you've never done. *Author—Unknown*

- "Seek first to understand, then to be understood" *Stephen R. Covey*

- Transform your mind, and go get your stuff! Get your blessings—the things that God has promised you. He is not a God that HE should lie.

- What you want is waiting for you. LET IT HAPPEN! GO GET YOUR INHERITANCE! WHY! BECAUSE IT IS YOURS!

- Yes, life may deal you a lemon sometimes, but you must never, never, never quit or give up. If this little girl, Chelby Cymone Terrell, can keep the faith during those difficult times in her life, surely we can have hope for better days.

*How "bad" do you want better days,
better times, and a better life?*

AUTHOR'S BIOGRAPHY

Brenda A. Parker
Inspirational/Motivational Speaker
Author
Trainer/Facilitator

www.theinspirationalwoman.com

Brenda Parker is a powerful, dynamic speaker, who is respected for her ability to captivate, inspire and motivate members of her audience to make immediate changes in their lives—by being the best that they can be in every area of their lives. Brenda has a love for people and desire to encourage them to live life to its fullest. Her vision and assignment is to impact the world with the WORD of God in an excellent way.

Brenda has a Bachelors of Science degree in Business Administration and Masters of Science in Human Relations and Business. She has over 20 years of experience in business, training and professional speaking. She co-authored with other business professionals the book entitled "How to Achieve Unlimited Success". Audiences say things like, "She is enthusiastic and confident", "Brenda's message is stimulating and thought-provoking", "Her enthusiasm is contagious", and "We want her to come speak again".